BUSINESS ENVY: 101

WHAT BUSINESS STUDENT

NEEDS TO KNOW

Marilyn Bryant-Tucker, MBA, EGCBA

BUSINESS ENVY: 101
WHAT BUSINESS STUDENT NEEDS TO KNOW
Copyright@2015 by Marilyn Bryant-Tucker.
All Rights Reserved.

Email: info@mbtmarketingsolutions.com

Ordering Information:

Quantity sales. Special discounts are available on quantity purchase by corporations, associations, and others. For details, contact the publisher at info@ mbtmarketingsolutions.com

Orders by U.S. trade bookstores and wholesalers, please contact MBT Marketing Solutions: Tel: (919) 345-2892 or visit www.mbtmarketingsolutions.com.

Printed in the United States of America

Book Design and Layout by
www.mbtmarketingsolutions.com
Marilyn Bryant-Tucker

ISBN-13: 978-1517380212
ISBN-10: 1517380219
Library of Congress Control Number: 2015915476
CreateSpace Independent Publishing Platform, North Charleston, SC

ABOUT THE AUTHOR

Marilyn Bryant-Tucker, MBA, EGCBA is the owner of MBT Marketing Solutions, and can offer quite a wide range of high-quality marketing services such as event marketing, branding, communication and much more. She is a certified marketer whom has great zeal for helping micro and small business owners grow their business, with her wealth of knowledge and experience. Bryant-Tucker is committed to giving the best of marketing services with a focus on reasonably prices, top-quality marketing and publicity services. She is a native of Rocky Mount, North Carolina, but for the past 27 years *of her life* resided in Raleigh, North Carolina. Marilyn holds an MBA in Marketing, Executive Graduate Certificate Business Administration and has pursued Doctoral Studies in Marketing. She earned her Master's Business Administration in Marketing from Strayer University in 2011 and an Executive Graduate Certificate.

CONTENTS

DEDICATION

I would like to dedicate this book to my husband, Richard Tucker. I want to thank my handsome husband for being so patient, for sacrificing much of our time together so that I could focus on my gift. Thank you for loving me unconditionally and making me laugh.

I would like to dedicate this book to my Mom for prayers, supporting and encouraging me. You instilled great values and taught your children to have faith and believe. I could not have asked for a better mom or role-model.

For all of my loved ones who've gone on to a better life, especially Grand Mother Lillie Mae Bryant, Grand Father James Bryant and Father Fred Dupree-you are always close in heart.

My Father has played a major role in 'who *I have* become' because he always told me, 'I was beautiful and smart'. I believed that, because *my dad told me so.*

ACKNOWLEDGMENTS

To my sister Sandra for inspiring me to 'follow my gifts.' I used to work on Saturday's at her Boutique store and learned for the first time that a person can be *self-employed,* and could also become their *own boss.*

To my sister Teresa for collaborating with me for special event planning. She is a successful entrepreneur and I am so proud of her. She has always been professional and organized, and she has taken those skills to begin her own wedding–planning business.

I want to recognize Michelle Hendricks, who put up with me over the years talking about marketing. Thank you for always listening to me and giving me great advice on everything.

To my clients, you made it possible for me to work on my gift.

Lastly, thank you for ordering my book and reading.

INTRODUCTION

B *USINESS ENVY: 101 - WHAT BUSINESS STUDENT NEEDS TO KNOW* is designed to reach out to college and university business students. Being a business or professional success is wonderful, but there may be downsides you've never considered. One might learn the secrets of achievement in school, but coping with jealousy, or external attacks, is something you'll learn only within the pages of this unique guide. Standing out as an entrepreneur or leader in one's field may draw accolades from some, yet scorn from others. How does one manage 'haters', false rumors, and personal onslaughts? These are certainly not topics covered by any class or discussed by most professors. However, they are common in the business community, and if expected and understood, such negative instances can be dealt with more effectively.

Business Envy: 101- WHAT BUSINESS STUDENT NEEDS TO KNOW covers the following:

- Cyber-bullying
- Understand your self worth and value to the business
- Coping with jealousy
- Tips for handling haters
- Includes a Strategic Marketing Plan Template
- Bonus chapters on basic marketing to better build your brand
- And much, much more...

Running your own business is often difficult, but not for the reasons you might think. Most believe the biggest challenge is having enough money or finding enough customers. Not so. The biggest challenge you will face as a business owner is marshaling your resources, and the key resource is time.

If you spend time on anything but doing what it takes to build and grow your business, you are actively fighting your own cause. As the CEO of the company, your time is at a premium. In fact, your time is supreme. Even five minutes devoted to something other than the two or three key things that will build a customer base and growing revenue is five minutes spent on the wrong things.

In matters of competition, being distracted by petty disputes of any given business day, many CEO's make the mistake of actually paying attention to things they a) have no control over and b) can't help them even if they did.

Until you can afford to hire the fire-breathing executive secretary who will keep distractions off your desk and out of your office, you have to evaluate everything in the following terms: if someone asked the President of the United States' staff to allow them five minutes to explain this problem in the Oval Office, would the White House staff allow it? If not, then ignore it. You are the president. Your job is presidential things. You don't park cars.

TIPS ON HOW TO HANDLE JEALOUSY

"Jealousy is when you count someone else's blessing instead your own blessing."

What is jealousy? Jealousy is several things actually and can play out differently within different people. It can *pop–up* as an emotional outburst, laced with malice and negative feelings that are a result of personal failure. Someone may be comparing themselves against other associates and successful people and then suddenly a thought arises within, and they begin to behave neurotically because of that insecurity. They have feelings that they will never be on par with those that are doing better than themselves.

Getting jealous is part of our lives; if taken in the positive aspect it livens up the competition. But when the feelings' extend too far, causing avoidance and insults, accusations and ridiculing, it becomes necessary to take positive steps towards handling those people.

Over the years, I have been networking with micro business owners, and have experienced jealousy and hatred from other business owners. These business owners remind me of kids in grade school and high school. They create their own networking groups and if they do not like you, they'll enlist other people to get on board with them, against you. If they see you as a competitor, or someone gifted, and looking successful, they don't like you. You have some that may act as if they like you, but they're only trying for what they can get from you.

Many business owners can be back stabbers and gossipers', trying to tear down other people. Some business owners don't realize, they can accomplish more if they learn how to collaborate, partner up and work together. They can become stronger in numbers.

So how *do you* interact with that jealous person, without being *burned*? Here are some ways to start with.

Take it as a 'compliment in disguise:' Yes; the best of compliments! You've gone from the mediocre, to genius! You must try to see the positive aspects and check what you've done so *brilliantly!* Was it something that you could not have achieved otherwise? Always work hard for further success; and never get depressed about being ignored, and certainly don't accept insult. I would say to you, be *proud* if someone is jealous of you and your achievements. This is a *great* compliment.

Knowing the person can help: If it's at all possible, get to know that person whom is jealous of you. In most cases, jealous people are not really known to you, they may be hiding their jealousy. They will probably resort to such activities as they feel threatened or afraid of the unknown, and when your brilliance escalates you through to your achievements, this only makes them even *more* jealous. However, it is very likely that when they are acquainted with you, they will evaluate you from a completely different angle and find there is nothing to fear, and then you are no longer a threat to them.

Either face up to them, or be invisible: When people become jealous of you, it may not be *you* personally they are jealous of, rather, it's more likely to be your status or situation they imagine you to be enjoying. Everyone is different and unique and no two situations are the same: and therefore, no single solution will work the same for all. I would recommend, that if you feel it's possible to get through to that person, confront them, and explain the situation. Try to work out *together* a possible solution. If you are both on the same page, and both understand each other, then many problems will simply disappear. Otherwise, if this will not work, then it'll probably be better to block them off and isolate yourself from them.

Judge the situation: Sometimes jealousy arises out of a typical situation. It is just like the man who does not treat his friends equally and thus unknowingly, he makes two of his friends, (that do not know each other) jealous. In such cases, bettering the situation by taking away your feelings for them, would help to remove the jealousy. But for those people who are envious and want to reach the top, no matter *who* they hurt along the way; just forget them! It is not possible to solve *their* situation.

TIPS ON HOW TO HANDLE HATERS

Have you ever been in a situation where you know you've done all you know to do, you've tilled the soil as such, worked the grounds, built the rapport needed; ultimately sealed the deal. But someone else comes along and simply plucks away your hard work, and takes the deal for themselves? How did that make you feel? Angry, annoyed and resentful? Probably, and *more* too.

Unfortunately, these things do happen in the work place, in the business world and in our personal lives. But how you handle it is what will bring you out on top, or pull you down into the mire.

I have been a marketing consultant for many years, creating success for myself and also many others I've been privileged to help. We can get battered and bruised by competitors that are *full–on* into making themselves come out tops, but at the expense of others; aka, myself included. They don't care, they will walk all over you and then spit you out again. But this is a poison, it will create grief where grief should not be. If you let it churn in your spirit and if you meditate on it, well: you have lost already. And it will only be a matter of time before the poison affects your market share and your own performance. The fantastic entrepreneur that people know you as already, will start to show–up cracks, and the cracks can only get bigger and more volatile for your business. This is the real battle. This is where you don't want to be. And this is what you need to do about it.

Talk to others and get some advice and moral support, don't hold onto it; let it go.

Keep a positive attitude and your conscious clear because the people you come into contact with, could perhaps be your next big sale or promotion; and they will detect a clouded conscious.

Keep doing the right thing, and if you can, enlist others to help you along the way. For example, join a business persons' network group in your community. Giving other business people sound leads within their expertise will reap a reward for you, in *your* field of expertise. The old saying . . . *you reap what you sow* . . . still rings true today; so by sowing good seed to another business person, this is going to bring good seed back to you. And if you still have a tinge of *revenge* against those that have harmed you, then rest assured . . . *they* will reap what they sow too. It is not your problem!

Setting goals will give you a desire to push on, and help you to *switch–off* things that can be a barrier and a hindrance. Set daily, weekly and monthly targets and do an audit on yourself from time to time; asking yourself questions like . . . "could I have done this better? What worked in this situation, what didn't?" Even if you determine only to make — say — a 2% improvement on what *has* been, then soon this would have escalated into a 10% improvement overall, and further down the track . . . a 20% improvement; the sky is the limit!

It's much harder to pull someone *up* onto a chair, *up* to your level than it is for someone to pull you *down* to their level, and to their low– life living. Determine not to become jealous, or covet other peoples' success. *You* are the greatest thing that could happen to your customers, *you* are the right person for the job! Good luck!

HOW TO HANDLE RUMORS

So, you've found out somehow that *someone* has been trying to defame you or your business, and it could very well hurt your reputation if you don't get to the bottom of it. Has that happened to you, or someone else you know? It may be more common than you think; in fact it's so common that I'm *sure* this has happened to you. Am I right?

There are many different reasons why people set out to hurt others, on purpose, and sometimes without purpose, they may not even realizing it! A lot of this can do with the fact, that people don't actually *have* the facts, they simply *assume* something; and they think they may have *heard* something about you, and then get all excited about it, because people *love* to gossip. Now you've heard the saying that . . . *assumption, makes an ass out of you and me,* haven't you? It surely does.

So, what do you do about it then? Well, you really need to look after yourself; preserve your good reputation by being consistent, and unwavering. Don't fall into the trap of . . . *He says, she says* so it must be true. *You* know the truth, and if your conscience is clear than the chances are that the *he says, she says* will eventually be forgotten about. This is one matter that should come out into the light fairly smartly and without too many ripples on the water.

Now, when people have a *malicious* intention and a *passionate* hatred about you or your business, this is a completely different matter! You need to take things like this seriously and find out the details *and* the source. Have a look and see why this accusation or intent has actually transcribed. Is there some truth in it, or is it just *plain–as–day* wickedness?

Truth will always trump deception, and the beauty about truth is that you don't need to *remember* any of the *lies* that have lead up to that situation which is relevant. You can *stand firm* against the tide, the ripples and the waves that might come against you.

Gather the facts, and then use them as a weapon. And if court action is required; if trespass notices need to be enforced, whatever, then build your arsenal and get some advice and support.

My mother used to say that you need to *get the big guns out*, to sort this thing out. What she meant was, you need to get the law involved, or the local government department, or even the *newspapers.* If you put your *plea for help* out there, or your *small claims court* application in, then you release the power of the law; and then you can sit back and forget about it. Don't lose any more sleep over it: let it go, and it *will* be resolved.

Now I'll leave you with this quote which I *love* from Rev. Rodney Howard–Brown, it just *nails* those rumors right on the head . . . *Opinions are like armpits, everyone has them and some of them stink!*

WHEN PEOPLE STOP TALKING TO YOU

Have you ever been in a situation where you have had what you thought, was an unshakable relationship; whether it were a business relationship, or a personal one? But suddenly you realize for some reason, it has all but disappeared. If you have, then you will probably relate to the fact that you begin to reflect, and wonder: what happened, and when; and why has it taken me this long to realize?

It's times like these that you need to do an audit on yourself, and try to uncover just *what* has happened. Look back to where your last contact with that person, or organization *was*. For some of you, you may know *exactly* when that connection went *pear–shaped*. It might have been a business or personal disagreement or a fallout, or a change of direction, whatever? But for others, it may not be so obvious.

At times a friendship, business relationship, partnership or collaboration *can* go bad. Some people simply cut you off without giving a reason. And you might feel you are to blame for that, you might even be angry about it.

Ask yourself, what sort of relationship '*did* we have then?' Was it a *giving* relationship; one that encouraged me, inspired me? Was it a relationship that was a two–way street, for example: did they listen to my advice, and did I listen to *theirs*? Or was it more of a . . . taking relationship? Did they suck out of me my energy and services, drain me and then give nothing in return? And, dare I say it . . . was the shoe on the *other* foot; were *you* doing that to them? After all, none of us are perfect: but so long as we remain teachable throughout our lives, then we should be okay.

We must respect *all* our relationships, whether they are good connections, competitive ones or not–so good ones. Sometimes we need to basically: agree to disagree; and that has potential to take its toll on any relationship; even to a point of *severing* them completely.

However, there are many others connections, relationships that we *should* still keep, because who knows what awaits us further down the track. Some relationships are actually *divine* connections, important connections that we will need later on down the road of our lives and business streams. These, are well worth restoring and holding on to.

So just what can you do to regain those *important* relationships? It's easy really; just reach out. Yep, as simple as that. Give them a call, search for them on *social–media* sites, find out what has gone wrong, and see if that relationship, (those *giving* one's is what I'm talking about) are able to be re-kindled and restored. If it's worth holding on to, then *go get them* again! And if you're a *die–hard* person, you might even look at restoring some of those draining ones, those hard to maintain ones. But so long as you have your good reasons for that sort of thing, it could be well worth the effort in the long run. As I said before, we are not perfect; no one is. Just so long as we remain teachable, we should be alright.

BUSINESS CYBER BULLYING

The world of the great matrix (www) can be a lot of fun, and you can literally share anything instantly with a large audience. You can swap photos and comment on people's blogs or learn much, and follow anything that interests you.

Every day there seems to be popping up a new *social networking* group that will tell you 'they're the best,' and you 'won't be able to live without us'. You can make lots of friends and create whole, different (virtual) realities. *Anything* can be put out there for all sorts of reasons, whether it be for revenue gathering or information sharing, whatever. And some even have very unsavory reasons why they create and try to attract others to their sites.

There are indeed unsavory people on-line who will try to woe you to their part of the world, or any world actually; after all, the www is *virtually* unlimited. There are *sharks* in the w-w-waters of the internet; and this very thing is what we are going to talk about today. A dirty word that can, and indeed *has* ruined people's reputations, businesses, friendships, lives and even *stolen* whole identities; *cyberbullying*. Yuk!

Cyberbullying can start off very small, subtle even; un-noticeable. A common tactic is someone will be-friend you, make you feel special, encourage you. Soon you feel safe with this person and familiar. Sometimes though it can be very blatant and boldly–disgusting! Awful really. How can this be?

Well, being a virtual world, you don't actually have to be yourself; you can be a completely different person and who would know? I've heard of men, or women even, who have posed as teenage girls' (here's a clue, people with devilish intent usually create a character that is in fact . . . their perfect target!) They create a whole new realty which is actually–a fantasy world. They become someone they are definitely *not!* They become a 'wolf in sheep's clothing,' looking to whom they can devour and destroy; looking to blackmail someone into something that is *totally* against their own nature.

I have had a personal experience of cyberbullying; when it first occurred, I didn't know what it was. It made me feel hurt, afraid for my reputation. All I could do was try and figure out how *did things get this far?*

People should be able to talk as adults to resolve individual problems, and to cry out for help before it's too late. Another thing I have experienced is people on social networks that don't like your posts, or don't even commenting on them. These may be people you have networked with and know you personally; but for some reason, they un–follow you, or gossip and try to cause *others* to un–follow you. I know this is not a big thing, but it *can* be! It can really hurt sometimes.

Just be very careful out there on the w-w-waters because there are some rocks in the way, bent on deceiving you, for some selfish gain of their own.

VARIOUS FORMS OF CYBERBULLYING

- **Belittling** – presenting unfeeling gossip aiming to soil some-body's or business reputation;

- **Trolling** – inciting individuals to outrage so as to get them to react improperly

- **Flaming** – utilizing dirty, accusative, hostile language;

- **Outing** – discovering individual and humiliating information about an individual and utilizing this to coerce or harass them by undermining to uncover it online;

- **Phishing** – deceiving an individual into uncovering personal and financial information.

- **Harassment** – sending steady and perpetual pernicious and offending messages to somebody;

- **Stalking** – taking provocation to the level of intimidating someone's safety;

- **Impersonation or impinge** – a devil put on a show to be someone else online so as to get that individual in a bad position or discomfit him or her;

TIPS ON HOW TO HANDLE CYBERBULLYING

- If you are bullied, reply politely and respectfully, beg them if needed. It safeguards you and your business ultimately.

- Do not give out your passwords or personal information. Even your friends could wind up giving your passwords to someone who should not have them.

- Be watchful about what you write or what images you send or post because nothing is really private on the Internet.

- If you are using a site like Facebook on a computer in the library, log out before you walk away. If you don't log out, the next person who uses the computer could get into your account.

- If someone bullies you, don't respond. Bullies are looking for a reaction, and you may be able to stop the bullying if you ignore or block the person.

- Save any evidence of cyberbullying, print it out, and show it to a trusted adult.

- Report bullying to your Internet service provider, Phone Company, email provider, or the website where it happened. Sites like Twitter, YouTube, and Instagram have online forms for reporting.

- Report cyberbullying to an appropriate law enforcement agencies.

TURN UP YOUR GIFTS

Young people *need* to be inspired and if parents can *see* their children gifts, then they should help them and encourage them, and nurture those gifts. As a child, I had an entrepreneurial spirit; what a gift to possess, naturally! I remember having yard sales, selling M&Ms' and oranges: whatever I could get my little hands onto, I could market and make a success out of it. This was something automatic to my spirit and my nature. I was one of those people that could *sell ice to Eskimos'*.

We all have special gifting's and abilities unique to ourselves; not everyone can do what you can do. And not everyone will be happy about what you can do and what they *cannot* do. In fact, you may even have some people who really dislike you because of what you can do, and what they cannot. It's called jealousy. But here's the catch that many people miss . . . *they* will also have their own talents and abilities that *you don't* have! It's what they do with them that will either make a success out of them, or a failure. And this is just what I want to talk about with you today.

You can be your own best friend, or your own worst nightmare; and if people are jealous of *you* and *your* abilities, then that is not your problem, but theirs. Be sure it doesn't affect you negatively.

If you can play a musical instrument, or solve a math problem in a heartbeat, then do it! If you can catch balls or hit them with ease, then do that! But if you cannot walk a tightrope, or even stay on a horses back for more than a second, then don't!

Follow your heart; do what *you* can do in the natural with *gusto*. Let those that *can* ride a horse, ride a horse. Don't get on your *high–horse* and grumble about it (pun intended).

Bishop Noel Jones, may have said this . . . "If you don't have any haters, than you are not very gifted." What does that mean? Does that mean . . . if you have no haters, then you actually *have* no gifting's? I don't think so: we all have talents! No, I think it's more likely to mean . . . *you are not using your gifting's . . . there is no* evidence *of them. Perhaps you've buried them!* What do *you* think about that?

I remember mom sewing my cloths when I was in middle school and then through college. I would somehow be nominated every year, through my dormitory, for being the best dressed undergraduate at *Fayetteville State University.* My mom was *very* gifted; she would see that my sisters, myself and other friends and classmates were well looked after. She operated in her gifting's and it was evident. I would draw out the design and pick out the material, I didn't know that I was becoming a Fashion Designer. Were other girls jealous? I have no doubt!

I never forgot once, when I was at a big event and someone said this . . . *what you've got on, is so Phat!* I didn't know what that actually meant, and I could have been quite offended by such a statement; but my friends told me (thank God for friends!) he's saying *your outfit is hot!*

So work out your gifts, learn what you're good at: and let's make some haters out there! (Oh, and then send them to this book – so they can learn the good stuff that you're learning.)

RUN YOUR OWN RACE

Have you ever looked at someone else's business and thought, *I could do that, and I could do it better.* You probably could, but should you? Competition is good sure, but it can also take you away from the *real deal* . . . the people you are dealing with and the clientele that are familiar with *you* and what *you* offer! Now I'm not promoting that you should bow to everyone's expectations, far from it. No, I'm suggesting that, perhaps that business which you're looking at and thinking, *I could do better,* is already covering the particular need and there is in fact *another need* for you to fulfill.

Run *your* race; use *your* skills and abilities. Because if you try to be someone else than you will only ever be a *second rate* someone else. Be the best that you can be, and be the best at being *you*.

So many business owners try to keep up with other business owners and become distracted. Their focus is on their competitors, or business owners they're trying to beat, and not their own clients! Look out for your competition and even bounce off their promotions etc. Go so far as to even show your customers what *they* offer, and what you have, and why you have the better deal and benefits as it were. To be armed with the competitors' ammunition is a power indeed. This shows that you are *up to the plate* and know your stuff. This gives your clients confidence in who you are, what you stand for, and can even sew a little seed of doubt as to what your opposition may, or may not have or do.

"Don't get distracted by competing with others. Run your race. You have exactly what you need for your assignment. Learn to accept your gifts." said Joel Osteen, a prominent minister of our hour. And by accepting your gifts and talents, you will have the upper hand; you will do well and you will not appear false in any way. Because people can easily see through pretenses; and you don't want to be seen as someone not to be trusted. Trust goes a long way in securing business and creating repeat clientele. This is something we all can appreciate.

STAY RELEVANT

As a business owner, you should always keep up with the current trends in your business genre and also the competitions; constantly promoting yourself.

At times you may need to collaborate and partner up with others and use their unique skills and attributes to help yourself with staying relevant. Celebrities do this all the time. For instance, many singers promote themselves by singing something of their own or someone else's with a hot and current celebrity, and by doing so, they are staying relevant: re-connecting with the masses. A great example is Dancing with the Stars, and Celebrity Apprentice. Many stars we have not seen on the scene for years, suddenly start appearing on these shows. By doing this they obtain a lot of press, and many even get hired for commercials, or sitcoms. At times you have to reinvent yourself to up your game.

It's not too difficult to do, you just need to come up with an idea and take some risks with it. Try having a brainstorming session with like–minded individuals; think outside the square. Write some things down and expand on them.

I know of a person who had been involved with theater on a few occasions, doing shows and dramas, and even appearing on television commercials once or twice. Then life suddenly got too busy, and they had to pull away from their passion, and get onto the straight and narrow; raising kids and being a family man, working a normal 9–5 job etc. Not an uncommon story. But he still had the *passion* smoldering away inside, and it wasn't getting used; instead it almost became dead, which was a real shame. These things do happen; you may have had a successful business and were *going for it,* being successful, fulfilled and prospering. And then suddenly it's not happening so much; sales may be down, ideas may be lean: dwindling.

It's times like these that you need to get help and advice from those that *are* doing well, and are prospering in their own right. Don't copy them, but do something with their advice. I'm sure they would gladly offer you help, so long as you're not a threat or a competitor to them; and so long as you reach out and ask.

So what happened to this *thespian* that I mentioned earlier? Well, he reinvented himself. He looked at the skills he had, and a way to use them that wouldn't encroach on his new–found life and family. Now days you can find him *writing* those dramas he was once performing, and also he uses his acting skills to do something completely different to what he used to do. Now, he's using those skills for audio books, and voice acting. It sure takes up a whole lot less time than his previous, endless auditions, and production preparation of old. He looked outside the square, and did something different. There's an old saying that goes something like this . . . *if you keep doing the same things that you have always done, then you will always get the same results that you have always had.*

Look around, look outside your bubble and find a sparkle of difference. Then be proactive and check it out. I'm sure you will surprise yourself.

STAY IN YOUR LANE

What I have observed over the years is this, business owners don't realize their main focus should be running their own business; too many try to be the *jack of all trades* and only end up positioning themselves for failure. For instance, if you're not a graphic designer, don't try to be one as this will only hinder your branding. Sure, it's a good idea to learn *about* graphic design; but consult with the people who have their graphic design credentials down–pat.

Some business owners seek people who may be a business owner, and because they appear to be successful in their business, they obtain business advice from them. Business Owners should seek out people that have credential in the business industry if they wish to learn how to have a successful business.

If you're sick, would you go to a Doctor that has credentials, or go to one without them? It's the same with business; get involved *with* business professionals with credentials and experience. And let them be your guide. It's their niche; you concentrate on *your niche.* Stay in your lane.

If you need graphics, and you're are a novice graphic designer, hire a professional graphic designer; and learn from them. If you want your marketing material to look like the big boys, then you need pro-fessional graphics, not tacky graphics.

It's the same when it comes to photography for your business. Many people take pictures with their phones and wonder why the pictures don't come out–well, *professional*. Oh dear, some will even use those pictures for their branding and it will only make your business look very unprofessional. This is a trap to avoid.

I know people who have done just that, and unless you have trained eyes to see the errors, you will miss them completely. Try this little experiment and you will see what I mean . . . Imagine a brand of car; not one you're used to, but a different brand. For example, if you drive a Honda, you tend to see lots of other Hondas' on your way to work or town, or where–ever. But if you think about a European brand that you're not familiar with: say a Skoda, or a Mercedes. Do you ever see any of them? Probably not. Now pick one of these brands and then go for a drive just to see if you can find some. I'll bet you will see a whole lot more than you have ever seen before. Isn't that amazing?

Now why is that you may wonder? The fact is, those cars have always been there, only you didn't notice them until they became part of your world. But they have always been in the world of those that drive them. They will even be able to tell you that the indicator lights and the wiper switches are on the other side of the steering column.

My point is, you can have *knowledge* of things; photography, videography, graphic design etc., but to have *wisdom* about a product or service takes years to learn and master.

Stay in your lane, and you will see the whole road ahead more clearly.

KNOW YOUR VALUE

W hen I first began providing marketing services, I did some work for free and also bartered, offering my services to others in exchange for something of theirs. The reason why I chose to work that way at the time, was because I was in graduate school and then I went on to doctoral school. I helped many business owners grow, and have success with their planned events etc. The problem was, I wasn't making any monies myself; yet I worked tirelessly on their marketing campaigns', and branding; putting in all the effort, with no monetary returns.

Well it came to a point where I wanted to be compensated for my work with some financial substance, and why shouldn't I? Working for free is ok, for a time, and for certain reasons: but we should not camp there.

When I provided a price list of my services, and also invoices I had not received payment for: I learned to value myself. Up until that point, I was an easy target for abuse of services because I did not value my expertise. Now this is not an unusual story, people do it all the time: and not always with intention. Sometimes others just don't really *think* about what you have done for them and made the connection that, actually, what you have done (and wonderfully) must have been a real sacrifice for you to carry out. So when you learn that what you *have,* is actually valuable, and that others will need it in some way; then don't be shy: put some monetary value upon it. People will not mind paying for your work, and they will certainly *see* that you do earn it.

Don't undermine yourself and your special, unique abilities. Some people will be upset about having to pay for something that they could have . . . once–upon–a–time, had for free; but if those people do not make the connection and value your work, then let them go; they will only end up being a hindrance to your progress anyway. The last thing you need is to be burning the candle at both ends, for nothing!

We must do an audit on ourselves from time to time, we need to put in writing some ballpark figures of what we are doing and what it should be worth. If you don't really know where to start, well then start with how much you would actually like to earn over the year. Divide that up by months and weeks, and finally *hours.* Ask yourself, *how much should I charge per hour for my services?* And don't forget to throw in the expenses *after* you've come up with that hourly rate, or you'll come up short.

Value your time, and what you produce *with* your time. Put your stake in the ground, and others will value that time too, and also *you.* They will finally make the connection that, really you are helping them to achieve their goals: and as the old saying goes . . . *success, breeds success.* If they are achieving their goals, then you will too.

CHARACTER

A beaming character can make all the difference in marketing!

The legendary President of America, Abraham Lincoln, once said, "Reputation is the shadow; character is the tree." In fact our character is much more than what we would presume.

Many people are talented, and can woe the crowds with their abilities and feats, they can lead whole armies to a battlefield with their charisma and zeal. Talent can shoot people to stardom in quick succession, make them lots of money, and gain huge followings. But it's not people's talent that endures the fires–to–come, it's their character. Talent can take you anywhere, but it is only character that will (or will *not*) sustain you. When the overnight successes are opened up for all to see, the cracks will surely show.

Some people do not have good character. I remember my Grandmother telling me, *it's your actions that speak louder than your words.* This is so true; this has stayed with me throughout my life. We ought to listen to our grandmothers.

What is a diamond? It is a small piece of carbon that has survived massive pressures, over a long period of time. What is a mighty oak tree? It's a small nut that has stood its ground. Character is the same . . . character is simply, who we are when no one is looking. It's the core makeup of a person that sets them apart, and if your character has cracks, and if it's weak or has *secret little issues,* then they will only increase in size until eventually you simply *fall apart.*

Everyone in this world has character of some sort; we might say that Mr. X or Y does not have any character. Character may be considered as an evaluation of the inherent moral qualities of an individual. This includes qualities such as honesty, fortitude, empathy and many more. Character is determined by the existence of what we call virtues and the absence of the so called *social vices.* And before we come to any conclusions about the character of any individual, we must ensure the presence of good qualities, and also the absence of bad qualities.

The fundamentals of character

- **Trustworthiness:** One should not deceive or betray anyone, be reliable always, must implement what has been said and moreover have the courage to do the right things and stand by everyone.

- **Respect:** One must follow the golden rule that there would always be differences and learn to respect the others views. All disagreements should be dealt with patience to arrive at the best solution based on mutual respect.

- **Responsibility:** One should not hesitate to do what he is supposed to do. Must plan ahead and stick to the plan and always keep on trying.

- **Accountability:** One must set good examples being accountable for words, attitudes and deeds.

- **Fairness:** One must always be ethical, open minded and treat everyone fairly without blaming.

- **Caring:** One should also be compassionate & caring helping people in need and express gratitude to the helping friends.

- **Citizenship:** One must do his share for the benefit and betterment of the community and help to protect environment.

Character vs reputation

Character and reputation are distinctly different. While your reputation says what the people think about you, your character determines who you really are. Most of the people tend to believe what other makes them believe and thus enhance their fall. I can cite you hundreds of cases where the person involved was very reputed and worked seamlessly on the reputation but had terrible character. And when, through intimacy, the character became known, the person was completely ruined. So it is always better to count on character rather than on reputation because basing on character means you are working on the stuff that is inherent in you and not imposed by others.

TEN COMMANDMENTS OF BUSINESS

Growing a business is much more challenging than starting it. This is because of the various factors and their intricate interrelationship that influences the success of a business. But one must remember that success is a journey and not the end itself; the moment you feel that you have reached the end, it is better to give place to others for further growth of the business. One must also bear in mind that whatever business strategies one may have, all these start with customer and end with them. Therefore the prime aim of the business should be to enjoy customer satisfaction always. The following principles are very good to start with for a growing business.

1. **Let the customers be satisfied:** Whatever products or services you may be supplying it should meet all the stated and implied needs and always exceed the expectation of the customers.

2. **Let there be a brand strategy:** The product or services the business is rendering must focus on serving certain some needs of the customers. Most of the businesses achieve success by solving a specific problems rather than wide range of activities.

3. **Let the existing customers be happy:** Happy customers always contribute to the business. A business should never indulge in targeting new markets and chasing new

customers only. If you do this, there may be a crowd of new customers in front but will also have long queue of escaping customers in the rear.

4. **Let the reputation be guarded:** Reputation or brand image is the most precious gem a business can have. You cannot learn anything while you are talking. So, listen to the customers attentively to know their perception and never criticize the competitors.

5. **Let there be referrals:** Referrals are one of the most active marketing tools, especially for small business when there are minimum promotional activities. Only happy customers can give you referrals to get more business.

6. **Let there be no unhappy customers:** A business must ensure that there is no unhappy customers. There may not be many complaints, but there could still be unhappy customers who can do huge damage to the business, besides switching over. Be proactive to get customers perception.

7. **Let the customer be a part of the business:** Customers and their perception only determines the success or otherwise of the business. As such they should be treated as a part of the business giving all information to product changes.

8. **Let there be teams:** Team building is a must for any growing business. Only a dedicated team working for

common objective can yield success.

9. **Let there be review:** Periodic review of performance or strategies is of utmost importance to any business. It helps to know the bottlenecks creating deviations from the business targets. These have to be identified, analyzed and interpreted for taking appropriate measures for continual growth of business.

10. **Let courtesy prevail always:** A customer is the sole purpose of the business. He is not an intruder and not someone for arguing or matching wits. He should always be treated with extreme courtesy for success of the business.

Follow these and you will have results like let there be growth and there is growth!

MARKETING IS JUST LIKE PLANTING A GARDEN

I remember growing up as a child, and working in the garden with my grandmother. She was my sweetheart, and mentor. At the time, I did not realize how gifted and smart she was; I would sit in the garden, and watch her dig the dirt and put the seed in to grow watermelons, collards, cabbages, potatoes', cucumbers, squash, and so much more. At first and for *some–time* there was no sign that anything was happening within the soil, and you could easily forget that something actually *was*.

My grandmother would go into the garden several days during the week, and she would pull the weeds, and water the garden. She'd need to keep the pests out too; she would have to *tend* to it. And then weeks later – I could *see* the fruit and vegetables grow! What I am saying is this, your *business* is much the same as gardening.

Now before you can do anything within a garden, you have to first have a *vision* of a garden and then you will need to actually create a garden. You need to *break–ground* and prepare.

You will need tools and knowledge, advice and eventually, physical effort.

First, you will need to decide what it is you are going to plant, and is it the right season for it; even to the extent of – is it the right location and climate? Good luck trying to grow bananas' in the cold climate.

As it is in gardening, so it is in business. You will have to have a right marketing plan, and branding. You will need to do some research and come up with some strategies; find out who your target market is and if the unique business will be sustainable in your area.

Can you *see it?* Have you planned how you are going to go about creating it? Will you have the right know–how to actually grow it, and create an abundant harvest? Don't lose sight of what's happening within your soil; especially when times get hard. It often seems fruitless, to start with when creating a new business. Think of this time as an opportunity to test different things and try new systems, products or processes. Think of it as a time to fine–tune your crop and do a bit of grafting to get the mix just right.

Next, when you have broken-ground and you have all the tools, people and wisdom to continue, then you will need to *keep* it in good condition, and attract the right people to spend time and money in your garden. You will need to analyze your business–garden regularly. Promote some plants, and fertilize them, perhaps pull some plants out, to make way for other plants. Some of those plant could even be your staff . . . Oops, that's not fair! Well it is actually, especially if your staff has their own agenda, or they're not getting on board with *your* vision. This is *your* garden and *you* want it to be a success, don't you?

There is no point in growing it if it's just going to be neglected and waylaid. So be aware of pests and weeds that may try to creep into your business. These pests could be things like *apathy, laziness, bad-attitudes, poor follow–up,* and many others. It is a whole lot easier to *create* something, than it is to maintain it, so keep your finger on the pulse. And just remember that gardens take time to grow; they don't happen overnight. There is a saying which I saw on the side of a freight truck once; it said . . . *no one has ever been to the top of a mountain, unless they have climbed it.* This is so true. Don't expect to be at the summit of your business in a day, or a week, or even in a year! Good things, and things that are worth doing, take time.

NOW WHAT IS MARKETING?

Marketing literally means "communicating the value of a product, service or brand to customers, for the purpose of promoting or selling that product, service, or brand." So it is some kind of strategic attempt that you make sure to yield substantial business results. In short it is theme (the abstract part!) I am going to transform into real time benefits. Remember marketing is very simple. Even if I do not have the product or service readily available at hand, I can start marketing of the same. And this is what all the business promotion ads are doing round the clock.

How to do Marketing?

When I am baking a cake I have to follow certain recipes. Of course I can make variations with flavors etc. but the main recipe remains unchanged. This is also valid for making gardens. I can make raised beds, flat beds and many more but follow certain steps to have the flowers bloom. Marketing is as simple as that. Just make a plan including the expected challenges, analysis of the situation from all possible angles and having an alternative plan ready in case the first one fails to yield the desired results.

The Bottom Line

As I told earlier; marketing means creating permanent opportunity for the product or services and therefore I put stress on building scope of selling rather than the selling itself at the first stage. I prefer that you stop talking about yourself but tell the audience something they do not know. Simply speak their language and you will find marketing as slicing through cakes.

IMPORTANCE OF RIGHT MARKETING STRATEGY

Marketing strategies are essential to promote a brand and also to increase its use resulting tangible financial advantage. It includes many business activities including market analysis, launching of the products and targeting the potential customers. The business owners and executives therefore need to know the importance of the right marketing strategies for building target markets efficiently. These are always a part of the brainstorming process and include the price of the product or services, its distribution or implementation for making substantial changes in the bottom line of the business. There is nothing right or wrong in marketing. No rigid market strategy can bring success. Your strategy should be totally changed or amended based on the change in market and customer profile.

How to choose the right strategy?

It all depends on the group of your potential customers. If your brand is meant for the use of the busy executives, it is always preferable to go online and specially take the help of web contents because this can convey the right message to them in short time through displays.

For targeting the younger generation any or all of three will suffice, though advertising through visuals always attract the customer best. And for the retired, offline written content yields better results as this segment of potential customers always prefer to read hard copies rather than searching webs.

TRADITIONAL MARKETING VERSUES

SOCIAL MEDIA MARKETING

U nderstanding traditional and social media marketing becomes easier if we correlate these to our CD or DVD selection process. What we do when we enter a kiosk lending those for viewing at home. After brooding over for some time on series of the CDs and DVDs stock most of us ultimately select the CD we heard someone has viewed. But why it is so? The simple answer is that we do not trust what is printed on the CDs but count on referrals.

The virtual world

Present era is the era of communication when people are using internet and different apps for sharing and viewing information. This new way of communication has such an impact that the internet is now loaded with all sorts of information one may desire to have. Every moment millions of people are assessing the net and such user density made it as a tool of creating opportunity.

What is traditional marketing?

Traditional marketing is mainly advertisement based and dates back to the Egyptian civilization when papyrus was used for making wall posters. It is the much recognized type of marketing that are categorized as using print media for advertising the product or services, on air broadcasting through radio & television, direct mailing such as sending brochures and making telephone calls.

Social media marketing

It is the very recent form of marketing strategies that is based on gaining traffic through social media sites. It focuses on creating contents that attract attention and eventually shared by the reader on the social media sites. Social media marketing creates great impact and when done effectively can generate publicity and profits.

Traditional versus social media

Traditional market is a one way communication channel where there is no participation from the viewers and as such it does not engage the customers. On the other hand the word of mouth is the hall mark of social media marketing and therefore has great impact due to active participation of the many parties involved.

Secondly the customers have grown immunity to the advertisements and do not trust any brand because the traditional message does not allow the customers to react. On the contrary, social media marketing is based on recommendations from friends and acquaintances amplifying the message to create great impact.

Coming to this point if you start thinking that social media marketing is just posting the traditional marketing media on the social network, you will be grossly mistaken. There is more to it social media marketing as it involves active involvement of all concerned.

The inherent relation

Though humanizing of brands is important it can never be the end to all means. Though social media marketing can be utilized for gaining intelligence about the brand, it should act as an online extension of traditional marketing for yielding the best results.

EXPERIENTIAL MARKETING

When thinking of marketing, the average person will think of TV commercials, flyers, and radio commercials. The objective being to describe the benefits, features and characteristics, however a new approach to marketing allows for consumers experience the brand or product directly, creating a special bond. While many use experiential marketing in parallel with their traditional marketing campaigns, only some combinations have shown excellent results. Experiential marketing is most common in the form of an event, where it gives the company the opportunity to form long term connections with future clients.

Experiential marketing is often referred to as 'Event marketing', and is primarily because there is no better way to form a special connection between consumer and brand than in person at an event. While traditional marketing methods introduce a product and provide an idea of what a brand or product is like, event marketing allows the brand to create a special bond, which in turn creates loyalty and influence. Events come in several forms, each of which have their own benefits. Some examples include conventions, fundraisers, conferences, workshops, exhibitions, fairs, and much more. Grand Openings, for example, is an excellent way to start forming connections from the get go. They are commonly planned for new restaurants, as well as other establishments.

Planning these events require a high level of expertise and understanding of event marketing, and with the proper event planning, it can jump start a new business, or even revitalize a dying one.

VIRTUAL MARKETING

We all know that "ill news runs apace". But have we ever thought why it is like that? Let us look at the adage again. The inner meaning of this adage is that not all news runs apace. There are two words 'ill' and 'apace'. These two words are the cardinal points of viral marketing. The first word 'ill' is the cause and the second word 'apace' is the effect. Now if I ask why it runs apace; the prompt reply would be that it is ill. But what this is actually about? It means that anything to have probability to run apace must trigger emotions. So is the case of viral marketing. It must be able to trigger emotions of the viewers to run apace which in internet marketing is to be viral.

What it is?

It refers to marketing techniques that produces exponential increase in brand awareness or attain other marketing goals. This is a self-replicating process analogues to the spread of viruses. While the simplest viral marketing was like spreading rumors by whispering campaign, on the realm of internet, it stands for the marketing techniques that influence the websites and/or the users to pass on specific marketing information to other sites and/or users for enhancing the visibility and effect of the message. In such strategies of marketing the message appeal to individuals with high social networking potential or SNP for further transmissions so as to reach a great number of audience in a very short period of time.

How does it work?

As amoebas can grow in numbers by cell division, viruses can also replicate themselves continuously in doubling the number in each generation as below.

O

OO

OOOO

OOOOOOOO

OOOOOOOOOOOOOOOO

OOOOOOOOOOOOOOOOOOOOOOOOOOOOOOOO

And their population surpasses all imaginations in very few generations!

Basing on this viral marketing involves communicating marketing messages to others creating opportunities for growth by attracting prospecting viewers. When carefully planned this yields very good results.

How to create a viral campaign?

Though each and every marketer wants the campaign to go viral, it is really impossible to predict which will go viral and which will flounder. However following these basic steps can increase the probability of the campaign going viral.

- **Making it visually appealing:** Even if the message is primarily text based, a compelling video must be added that matches the product or services.

- **Planning the campaign:** Most of the successful viral marketing campaign is carefully planned. The campaign should include a good iconographic for clear communication of the message.

- **Tickling emotions:** To go viral the campaign should tug on emotions of the viewers and as such they must be designed with emotional catches.

- **Knowing the audience:** The campaigner must have clear ideas about the target audience and the emotional triggers required to awaken them. Moreover, it is also important to know when they are most likely to be online visiting social sites and launching the campaign at the appropriate hour.

- **Making it simple and casual:** Never try to force anything on the viewers. They have their own sense of judgment and therefore your campaign should be simple and with a carefully planned casual approach.

WHAT IS BRANDING?

A brand could be a name, content, design or any other feature that distinguishes a product or service putting the same ahead of the other products. This process involved in creating a permanent impression for a product or service in the consumers' mind is called branding. It is created through continuous advertisements promulgating a consistent theme to attract customers and also to keep them loyal.

Why branding is essential?

Be it a spa or, restaurant branding is very important. In this present era of tough competition, branding has turned to be absolutely essential, necessary and vital. For any product or services right branding helps in delivering a clear theme, promoting recognition, confirming the credibility of the product or services in the minds of the consumers connecting them emotionally. Branding is more than a logo or graphic design. When one thinks about the brand, he or she in fact remembers the entire customer experience, that is, it is the way the consumers perceive the business. Further it motivates the buyers and keeps them glued to the product or services.

Right Branding Adds Values to the Products or Services

We all have names and we are identified by those. But what are those? In simple terms these develop emotional connection and trigger some inner switch to respond. When we hear the phrases 'COCA COLA' or 'DIET MOUNTAIN DEW' these trigger our mind to remember the satisfying drinks and the series of adventures. Brands are simply like this. It triggers us, attracts us and motivates us to have the product. As it is said that seeing is believing, the brands do just the same thing. Therefore a high resolution and relevant logo is important. Using a logo that has no connection with the product will ever be able to influence the mind of the customers and draw them towards the product. With the right selection of image, content, fount and colors, the product or service is sure to register in the consumers' mind and attract them to use the same.

SWOT ANALYSIS

When staying alone I had to manage all my daily chores from cooking to cleaning. You won't believe that it took me several eggs to learn just how to boil eggs perfectly. In the first attempt the eggs were less than half boiled and next time I let it boil more ending with an almost dry pan and the egg with cracked shells was somewhere between boiled and burnt egg. After tracking back the process followed in my mind I found that I have ignored certain basic principles. I have employed all my strengths like applying heat for boiling water but did not consider the fact that boiling for long hours will evaporate the water. Then I started looking for alternatives and after thinking for another couple of minutes I adjusted water and heat with constant vigil and eventually got a boiled egg for my breakfast. Later that day I came to the conclusion that if I have planned the process considering the helpful and harmful elements, then in all probabilities I would have been successful in the first attempt.

What is SWOT?

It is the abbreviation of **STRENGTHS, WEAKNESSES, OPPORTUNITIES & THREATS.**

SWOT planning is a structured process of planning that takes care of all these four elements in any process for achieving desired results. Out of these four elements Strengths and Opportunities are helpful elements for achieving the objective and weaknesses and threats are the harmful elements hindering achievement.

How it can help?

SWOT requires nothing but a little thought. If done properly it has the power to uncover hidden opportunities for exploitation and when the weaknesses are clearly understood it makes you alert and you can eliminate the threats. This simple technique is equally applicable in all processes and when applied in the context of business projects, it helps to have an edge over the competitors due to its inherent property to reduce failures. It can be used as a starting kit and also as strategic tool in making business decisions. In fact for my every planning of personal and business projects I resort to SWOT analysis.

How to use it?

SWOT is a kind of self-analysis. It is best done by preparing a checklist containing questions on all the four elements of SWOT. These questions should be answered to generate meaningful information and brainstorming has to be done to do SWOT analysis.

There is again a crux. In any business process the Strengths and Weaknesses are often your internal factors or the hard realities and the Opportunities and Threats, the abstract ones, are mostly due to the external factors. In every business you have to see how both the internal and external environments match.

Opportunities may also arise from new technologies, further investments and the state policies. It is; therefore, always better to analyze the strengths and elements for achieving best performance. A good way to look at the opportunities is to revisit the strengths and weaknesses. You must try to find out if the strengths open up any opportunity and how you can create new opportunities by reducing, if not totally eliminating, your weaknesses.

And when you do this it will make you ready for eliminating threats. I would suggest that, after you are familiar with SWOT, you should try the TOWS analysis, in the reverse direction, treating external elements first.

TARGET MARKET

Learn how to reach your target market and niche to gain more consumers.

Creating a perfect marketing tool for reaching the target market and gaining more customers is not easy. It varies form organization to organization depending on the realities they are banking upon and the abstracts they want to achieve. Even a small business can create very strong and meaningful marketing strategy based on their specific conditions.

Let me tell you the story of a Japanese company that made the traditional Japanese screens for decorating and dividing rooms. As there were more and more modern apartments for contemporary living styles, there was an obvious recess in the market of the company. Do you know what they do? At the next trade show they recreated their workshop there and brought their traditional artisans who have spent their lives making ornamental screens to the trade show stall. The artisans started making screens in the stalls. At first nothing happened, but after some time crowed started to gather to watch the astounding intricacy and fascinating craftsmanship of the product. They did not brag or advocated their product but the silent show helped them to revive.

This strategy helped them and so you can make your own strategy to reach the target market depending on your exact condition.

WHAT IS A TARGET MARKET?

The target market actually means a specific cluster of customers that a business aim and evolve its marketing efforts around the group and finally sell their product or services to this cluster of customers.

How to define and reach the target market?

Even before you plan to launch any marketing campaign, you must know the target market. That is who will buy your product or services, how to appeal and persuade them. The following steps will help you in defining and reaching your target market easily.

- **Defining the target market:** As a gardener clear the weeds from the garden, you should also discard the 'maybes' first for keeping your marketing campaign focused and at the same time cost effective. It is better to stratify the target market based on demographics that is their personal details like profession, income etc. psychographics or their attitudes, values, likings etc. And behavior including their consuming habits.

- **Reaching the target market:** Once you are sure about the target market, you must find ways to reach them and the basic principle about this is 'fish where it is available'. If your target market consists of busy professionals of 25 to 35 years, you should try engaging them through social media and online activities. On the other hand if your target market is made of mostly retired people of 55 to 65 years, it is better to opt for printed materials as they love to read. Whatever line you may follow, you must ask the advertising managers to analyze profiles for effective marketing.

- **Identifying the types:** There many customers who always switch brands influenced by promotional offers. So you must be aware of the customers i.e. if they are your existing ones or new or the switching type to set your campaign accordingly.

- **Customizing strategy:** As you have the knowledge of the customers you must follow the appropriate method to reach, engage and also for gaining new customers.

IMPORTANCE OF WRITTEN CONTENT

Web Copy, Web Content, Written Content

Web copies are SEO friendly, short and best for sharing. These contain product description and inspirational thought about the product or services

Web contents comprise of aural, textual, <u>visual</u> <u>contents</u> encountered as a part of the user experience on <u>websites</u>. It may, among other things, include any or all of images, sounds, videos and animations.

Written content contains only textual description of the product or services intended to be promoted and usually published offline, through online written contents are also in use.

VISION, MISSION, & VALUES STATEMENTS

None of us can deny that messages are better conveyed through stories than hundred words. If I say "We must build a great organization for unleashing the creativity and focusing the corporate activities that will enable to develop the most efficient product or services in world. To offer our customers only the best and cost effective product or service with our state-of-the technology that will be energy efficient and environment friendly" and ask anyone to repeat it, I do not know if anyone would be able to tell. This is because it does not put a print on our mind and, therefore, how much informative it may be we really do not recognize the meaning and naturally will not be able to follow. Most of the vision, mission and values stamens are like that. Those stay there hanged but being purely ornamental is hardly of any help.

What are those then?

- **Vision statements** contain the objective of the organization based on economic considerations and are intended to provide guidance on decision making. A carefully crafted vision statement helps to communicate goals to employees throughout the organization.

- **Mission statements** convey the purpose of the organization and serve as filters to separate important from the unimportant ones focusing on the status, the activities and the purposes.

- **Value statements** inform the customers and the employees of an organization about the priorities and beliefs of the organization. These are used also for connecting the target customers.

Understanding Vision, Mission & Value Statements

Quite often these two are jumbled up though they are distinctly different. So, how to understand the difference? Let me tell you the best way to understand these clearly. To do this let us add 'ARY' to both of these words and see what happens.

Vision + ARY   = Visionary

Mission + ARY = Missionary

So, these two coined words now seem to be quite familiar as we know what these people do in the society. Visionary is someone who can see the potential of something like Jesus Christ who knew what was possible. The value statements describe the fundamental principles creating positive image of the organization.

How to write these?

There is no point in putting all the good words together as the example I cited earlier. These are like twitters and never help to achieve objectives. The vision, mission and values statements should be crafted in simple language making the future plans, stating what is possible and defining how it will be done.

SUCCESSFUL STEPS TO EVENT PLANNING

When in this present age of Instagram, Twitter, Face book, LinkedIn and when we can also share information using VoIP and webinars what could be the utility of holding customer events? Though the idea of holding events may seem to be outdated in the virtual world of communication; holding events is still a very strong way for improving customer relation and also for creating a buzz in the market.

I have specialization in event planning & event marketing and I enjoy doing it. Through my long exposure in this field, at last I learned that you require detailed planning and tight execution for making an event success.

Before I start dwelling on the stepping stones of event planning let us share a few words about events and their benefits.

Events and their benefits

Event can mean anything from social gathering, wedding ceremonies, school formals, festivities, conferences and many more. But for the purpose of marketing we shall confine our discussions on understanding a brand identifying target audiences, detailing the logistics and others for launching customer events. Managing events is used as marketing tools by many organizations, big and small. Events may also include elements like music & entertainment or specially chosen venue to influence the theme of the event.

How much you may communicate with your customers and clients in the virtual world, personal interaction has unique advantage of creating brand loyalty, generating referrals and increasing sales as well. These help to have direct interaction with the industry populace for sharing innovative ideas, opportunities and partnership.

The stepping stones

Like any other thing in your life events also require great amount of detailed planning involving the following steps.

1. **Developing the goal & objective:** You should be clear in mind why you are going to hold the event and what you expect to achieve out of it.

2. **Assessing the resources and constraints:** You should assess all your resources like the peers, staff members, community groups besides financial resources and must also identify the areas of hindrances.

3. **Organizing the team:** Events require concerted efforts and therefore you must form a team with members having experience in different aspects under the Event Manager. Members of the team should have allocated responsibilities of different functions like venue management, publicity management, sponsoring arrangement etc.

4. **Brainstorming ideas:** If you desire to have a unique event you must do sufficient brain storming on the theme and its implementation. All ideas must be accepted with equal importance so as to get the best out of those.

5. **Setting the date:** This is very vital as nothing succeeds without a target. But you must allow enough time for smooth implementation and check with the speakers and participants about their availability to make it a grand success.

6. **Branding the event:** Events should be branded with catching theme for success.

7. **Developing budget:** Consider all associated costs and sponsoring amounts for forming a realistic budget.

8. **Creating Master Plan:** These should include all administrative process of managing venue, registration, speakers, publicity & promotion, follow up dinners etc.

9. **Identifying partners and sponsors:** This includes finding corporate and community patronization for funds and organizing venues.

10. **Structuring evaluation process:** You must form tools to scaling the success of the events and the impact it created.

NETWORKING AND REFERRAL

I do not know how many of you have seen fishermen fishing with nets. When I first saw it in my childhood, I was simply taken aback seeing those getting fishes from under the water. But when I think of the same process at this grown age, it teaches me many things about network and referrals. But how? It is simple. Just try to trace back what the fishermen do step by step. They get their net – choose a spot – cast the net and after a while start pulling it out. The results: they find number fishes in the net.

As the fishes are stored, they repeat the process severally for more catches having idea of their daily requirement. Have you noticed any specialty of the process? Let me tell you that the fishermen never concentrates on the individual fishes as they can never guess what fish will be caught in the net but remain solely concerned over casting of the net.

Marketing through networking and referrals is same as fishing with a net. Like the fishermen who never have the idea of the size of the fish beforehand but knows that once caught it belongs to him and therefore focuses on casting only. Networking and referrals also give you no preconceived idea of your prospecting client but ensures that when someone comes, you can keep him loyal to your brand for business growth profitability.

What is networking and referral?

Networking is literally an activity that helps people to recognize, create and also take actions on business opportunities. And by referral we mean business promotion through third-party introduction. The primitive form of referral is the word of mouth and you can influence networking and referral for sustainable business returns by applying appropriate strategies.

Many of us have the misconception that the referrals obtained are due to chance factor only, and have no connection whatsoever with gaining new clients. Believe me, for networking and referral, what you say luck or chance factor is simply persistence finding opportunities. As such there should be continuous networking and referral activities for business prosperity.

Why networking and referral work?

Networking and referral are the natural outcome of everyday business activities. Though at the beginning it looks like to be chaotic, but this works well at the end .It works because of the reward the customer or the visitors get in return of referring people to your network. Suppose 'A' buys something from you, he gets a referral link for inviting others to your stores. Next 'B' receives email from 'A' with his referral link and buys from your stores and the cycle is repeated.

How to build referrals?

Third party endorsement is the most powerful vehicle for successful marketing. In every business a large number of clientele comes through referrals. Following tips will help to build a solid referral program.

- Identifying sources

- Adopting long-term approach

- Understanding the requirements and motives

- Creating a business group

- Taking care of the referral sources.

The Final Words

Networking and referral is the right step to keep growing as it saves time, enhance relationship and reduce marketing costs.

COLLABORATION AND PARTNERSHIP

We are stronger in numbers: collaboration and partnership

I think most of us are aware of the adage "United we stand divided we fall". But if asked to use this policy in their business activities, they fail miserably. Being stuck up with the age old hypothesis of competition they ignore the role of companionship as a great tool for achieving their goals.

Why collaboration is the key to successful marketing?

None can deny that there is strength in numbers. Brand partnership works through the loan of the brand equity. Brand collaboration helps to satisfy a period of time and function. Thus collaboration is not mere a strategy but the vital key for winning marketing battles for long term business growth.

Power of Collaboration and Partnership

Collaboration and partnership helps to overcome business challenges. It increases business effectiveness through joint marketing activities. It also helps to widen the marketing reach and utilizes the expertise of the professionals for group benefit. Further it works towards building of mutual trust and brings relevance, enhances creativity & resources for co-branding activities unveiling the hidden opportunities and decreasing the individual cost of marketing. Collaboration and partnership also help to arrive at the best solution in least possible time.

How does it work?

Having a brand partner is something like introducing your favorite 'X' to your pub mates. When you do so, you are unconsciously using endorsement options to get 'X' to reach new audiences. As you further engage with the group of your brand partner, the group becomes two times larger and naturally your marketing efforts and their effects also get doubled. It may also grow further depending on the effort of the group.

Setting Marketing Collaboration

Finding new customers is a challenging job every business face. Setting up strategic partnership for marketing is a cost-effective way to reach new audiences. The process of collaboration and partnership begins with identifying the goal. To be successful one also has to wear the customer shoes i.e. think like a customer. What are the brands the customers are interacting now? What they are aspiring for? And all such questions need to be answered from a customer point of view. Once this is done the next step is to focus on the relationship to make things happen favorably with a clear but flexible planning to achieve common goal. By amplifying partnership one can get better ROI.

Who to collaborate with?

This is very pertinent question and is apt rise in your minds. You can identify partners either through contacts or through networking. One can also take the help of experts who can align thoughts, agendas and expectations and once a prospective partner is found consider your mission, corporate social responsibility and identity for forming a strategic marketing collaboration.

ADVERTISING

Do you want to become a successful business person, with a thriving business? Then you will need to invest in your business. This is a no–brainer, for instance you will need to throw in a budget for advertising if you are to reach a wider target audience. Advertising can be a burden, but it is an essential part of the process. Regular advertising works better than something every now and then. People only *actively* see advertising when they're looking for something in particular, or if something catches their eye; so you may feel it's not really working sometimes. But *regular* promoting will bring you and your business to the forefront of someone's mind when they're ready, and in the market for something.

A fantastic way to advertise is to get involved with local groups of business professionals, regularly, even weekly. Groups such as *BNI, (Business Network International)* are fantastic! The business people that attend these groups effectively become your eyes and ears on the ground for you, and your business. They pass on qualified referrals' to you, and you will tend do the same for them. The philosophy behind it is called *givers gain.* Besides, advertising can usually be 100% reclaimable when the tax man comes–a–knocking.

You may have to hire staff to help run the business (hopefully you will *need* to, and many of them!). If you are trying to produce too much beyond your individual capabilities and enterprise and trying to do everything yourself, this could create bad customer service, and an unprofessional business result; you will effectively *hamstring* your business.

Don't be afraid of increase; in fact, reach for it. Some people hinder their own progress because they are scared of failure. If for example, you're a painter and you see advertised a large scale contract; we'll, do the numbers, put in your tender and get it! But make sure you cover all your bases, hire the staff you will need, and get that extra equipment you're going to have to have and then do the right thing: get stuck into it with gusto and professionalism. And, most importantly, produce quality results. If you don't, then that's going to really reflect badly on any future prospects.

Synergy is a powerful force; for example, one Clydesdale horse can pull about 2 ton, but two Clydesdale horses' together, can pull 8 tons'! Having staff on board, will drive you harder, and you will achieve much more. And if you achieve much more, than you can receive much more.

GOAL SETTING

You should set goals first for achieving success in everything.

C an anyone tell me what makes lives different? I know there will be hundreds of different stories. But when you summarize these, the basic reason comes out to be goal setting.

Let me tell you something about a business school. This is all about their students achievements. They selected groups of students and evaluated them based on their grades and future plans. The college further evaluated them 10 years after they have passed and came out with surprising findings. The study revealed that the most successful were not the students who used to achieve higher grades, but those who had specific future plans even 10 years ago. So, there lies the difference between the successful and unsuccessful people. To be successful one must have a goal and know where they want to go for reaching their ultimately. Obviously, the next question will be how to achieve goals? Like to visit a place you must know that place first, to achieve goals in business, personal life or events one should know how to set those first.

Focusing: the great tool

Most of us are unaware of the power of focusing and never really focus. We have the typical habit to concentrate on many things simultaneously and thus loose our eye from what we actually want to achieve. If a plank is placed on the floor and ask you to walk on the plank from one end to the other all of you will certainly be able to do the same quite easily. But if I place a plank connecting the roofs of two tall buildings across the street, hardly one or two will be able to make it. This is because most of you will start on thinking what will happen you slip and from fall from such a great height and thus losing the focus on the entrusted job. After setting the goal you should concentrate on that only and must stay focused always or achieving the target.

What are goals?

A goal is the desired result that any individual or business organization plan and engage to achieve within a definite time frame or deadline. This should not be mixed with visions which are most of the times unspecific and not

like staying healthy. But a goal is an aim that can be measured. Further it should be achievable. If you set a goal of topping the Everest without having mountaineering training, it can be termed as your dream but not goal because it is not realistic.

What are short term & long term goals?

Short term goals are the things that you want to do in the near future, may be a week, a month or a year, such as paying your credit card bills at the month end. These help you to focus on what you can do right away. Usually these are the parts of the larger targets and guide you towards achieving the long term goal. On the other hand long term goals are those you wish to achieve in the distant future. Usually these are the culmination of various short term goals achieved in parts. While the short terms goals are like making your credit card payments on time, the long term goal is to have good credit rating that will be helpful for securing further credits.

How to set goals?

You can best understand the short term and long term goals and what they are all about by following the limited over cricket matches when a team chases a target score. As they lose several wickets, they set their target of runs for every over for ultimately winning the match.

Effective goal setting determines how an individual or business will succeed. There are six golden rules of goal setting as below:

1. **Only set the goal that motivates you:** The goal should be important and relate to the high priorities in life. It should be able to push you beyond your present level and must have some values in achieving.

2. **Set realistic goals only:** To do this you should follow the 'SMART' principle. That is your goal should be **S**pecific, **M**easurable, **A**ttainable, **R**elevant & **T**imed.

3. **Put it in writing:** When you write the goal it becomes tangible and as you can see it always there is no way to forget the same. Moreover, when displayed it reminds you of the task ahead always.

4. **Make it positive:** Your goal statement should deal with what you want to do and not the things you do not want to do.

5. **Frame action plan:** Jot down all the steps and what you need to do in each step of the plan. Only by this you can realize if you are making progress.

6. **Make it flexible:** You should keep this in mind that setting goals is a way to achieve the target and not the target itself. As goals are always set over a time frame there should be enough flexibility to adapt to the changed situation but never losing the focus on achieving the target.

How to create SMART goals

- A Specific goal has maximum chances of achieving success. To frame this you should take the help of the six Ws. You must question who is involved? What will be accomplished? Where it will be done? When it will be done? Which will be fulfilled? And why it should be done?

- The **Measurable** goals allow you to know your performance. For doing so you must ask questions like: How much? How many? How to know if it is achieved?

- To make your goals **Attainable** you must chalk out various ways to make it happen including development in attitudes, skills, improved technologies and financial assistance.

- The goal set must be **R**elevant to your periphery of work. You can make it as high or as low you may wish for framing the long term and short term objectives respectively.

- Nothing should be left for indefinite period as in such cases the goal set loses its importance and urgency. As such goals should always be **T**imed.

WORKING AGREEMENTS

Working agreements alleviate confusion and reduces risk.

All of us shake our hands for so many reasons. But do you know how it started? Whether you believe it or not it started first to ensure one another that neither of them was carrying any weapon. And as the meaning of everything changes with time, handshaking is now evolved as a contractual symbol indicating complete agreement between the two persons.

It is now pertinent to ask if the handshake deals still carry some weight. Over the years I was also an ardent follower of handshaking principles. It never struck that it could be dishonored. But well, experience is the learning we all receive from our past mistakes and I am no exception too! Now whenever I do a job I put every detail in writing and get those signed by the concerned parties before starting the job. Now I have no fluctuation as the working agreements alleviate confusion.

The realm of promises

Promises are in fact contracts expressed by spoken communication and not written down. If there is an oral promise about doing something and finally not doing that, it is also a breach of contract with the only specialty that this is difficult to prove in the court of law. But when these are available in the written form it becomes absolutely easy to call for specific performance of the same.

The working agreements

The inherent advantage of this is that it not only states the promise made, but also serves as a token of proof. Being the promise and proof simultaneously working agreements are more ironclad than oral contracts as these are made by and between the parties. As these contain the signature of both the parties it ensures that both of the parties clearly understand what is stated and are committed to comply the stipulations.

The zone of trouble

When it comes to one person's spoken words against the others, it may be absolutely difficult to find the justice in case of any broken promises. Working agreements may also cause future problems because of poor drafting. But it is still better for minimizing the risks of violation.

Advantages of working agreement

Let me tell you some of the inherent advantages of working agreement in the following lines.

- **Preventing amnesia:** Jotting down the deals means you have to keep nothing in mind and so there is no chance of a slip causing confusion and conflict.

- **Easy reference:** Working agreements help to provide handy reference for answering any queries about the details.

- **Planning the work:** Putting details in writing is a great way to have a well thought plan about the job and the responsibility of the parties.

- **Encouraging consistency:** Having everything on paper means providing uniform set of information to all concerned and thus increases consistency of performances.

- **Promoting harmony:** Working agreements prevent disputes. These also act as a guideline and play a very vital role in resolving potential disputes or confrontation.

- **Easier enforcement:** Working agreements are easier to enforce because of its absolute legality.

- **Sealing the deal:** Working agreements seal the deal in respect of time, cost, commitment, responsibility, compensation thus lead to smooth implementation.

Up Your Game:
It's Marketing Made Simple

WORKBOOK

MARKETING ONE PAGE PLAN TEMPLATE

DEFINITIONS

Target Market

Target market is basically the potential buyers to whom a business wants to sell its products or services, to which the business diverts all its marketing campaigns and those who are likely to buy products or services from the business. Marketing strategy of the business is based on this element and this can be separated by several factors like location, buying capacity and demographics.

A niche market is the subset of Target Market. There can hardly be any business that can cater to the needs of all people meeting all of their requirements. As a matter of fact narrow marketing has greater chances to grow. Target Niche may be defined as the part of the target market where the business concentrates to separate it from competitors. This is a subset of the Target market on which a specific product is focused. There is no existence of target niches in the market, but these are created by the business identifying the requirements. This makes the business cost effective and also helps to operate more effectively.

Positioning Statement

Also referred to as brand positioning statement, it is a succinct expression of how a given product or service fulfills the needs of the consumers better than the competitor brands. There are four elements to this: Target customer, referential frame, Point of difference and convincing reasons. A good positioning statement helps to identify the appropriate niche and also to get established in the market.

Offering to Customers

In marketing offering to customers means your ways to make them understand the sum total of benefits they receive for associated payment in using your product or services. It helps to enhance the customer's perception of your products or services affect their decision for purchasing from you.

Price Strategy

It refers to the method a business applies for pricing their products or services. This takes into account various segments like paying capacity, condition of the market, action taken by the competitors, costs and margins. There are many types of price strategy such as discount pricing, penetration pricing, price skimming, product life cycle pricing and competitive pricing.

Distribution

It is the process that a business employs for spreading the products or services throughout the market, for consumption, directly or through intermediate channels. This is critical for every business and the businesses moving faster and wider than the competitors makes more impacts and enjoys greater margin.

Sales Strategy

A sales strategy focuses on the efforts of a business for improving sales focusing on the existing and potential target customers and communicates with the market in appropriate ways. It includes a plan that helps the product to gain advantage over the competitors. All successful sales strategies have a defined sales plan, sales activities, targets and timelines.

Service Strategy

It aims to optimize the after sales service that a business provides by coordinating components, service personnel and service cost. Such strategies help to gain customer loyalty through improved after sale service performance.

Promotion Strategy

It is the process of getting the brand public for attracting potential customers. It uses a blend of advertising, personal selling and public relation for promoting the products or services. The promotion strategies differ depending of the specific needs of the business, but all of them strive to enhance brand awareness and demand.

Market Research

It is the organized effort employed by a business for collecting information about the target markets and customers. It includes social and opinion research analyzing and interpreting the information gathered for effective decision making. It helps you reduce the risks and also helps to focus on the resources where those will be most effective for producing desired results.

Other Component of your Marketing Plan

Any marketing plan has five 'P's: product, price, promotion, people and place and the other components of marketing plan include mission & vision statement, situational analysis, budget and action plan, metrics, monitoring of results.

Paws Doggie Day Care 2015

Marketing Theme: Fun without the Sun	
Category	**Strategy**
My reason for existence:	To provide pet owners within the city of Springfield a safe and fun place for their pets
What sets my business apart from the rest:	An indoor pet park and pay-land
My ideal customer is:	1. Springfield professionals working in the 10 mile radius 2. 3.
What's most important to my ideal customer when they are buying what I'm selling	1. That their pets are safe 2. Pets can have fun in any weather 3. Exercise
What I want to accomplish this year:	• Lease a building • Recruit customers •
The top 4 things that are going to get me there:	1. Direct mail in nearby developments 2. Drop-offs in office parks 3. Open house events 4. Social Media Marketing
How much will each program contribute to my revenue/profitability:	1. Mail - 30% 2. Drop offs - 15% 3. Open House - 25% 4. Social Media Marketing 30%
What will trigger my ideal customer to think of me:	• Being stuck at work and pet needs to be let out • •
Programs I am running to reach my goal	1. Online Advertising 2. 3.
How much money will I need to get it done?	1. $2,500 2.

YOUR COMPANY NAME HERE 2015

	"THEME"
Category	**Strategy**
Target Market	
Positioning Statement	
Offering to customers	
Price Strategy	
Distribution	
Sales Strategy	
Service Strategy	
Promotion Strategy	
Marketing Research	
Any other component of your marketing plan	

BOOK DISCUSSION QUESTIONS

1. What is the most important point the author is trying to make in her writing?

2. What was your favorite part of the story?

3. Which of the chapters you like best? Why?

4. Have you encountered some of the problems and situations?

5. What one thing would you recommend to a business owner?

6. How would you describe business envy?

7. What resources does the school offer to help students launch a business?

8. Do you plan to become an entrepreneur or work for a company?

9. How do you measure business success?

10. How do you measure business failure?

ABOUT THE AUTHOR

Marilyn Bryant-Tucker, MBA, EGCBA is the owner of MBT Marketing Solutions, and can offer quite a wide range of high-quality marketing services such as event marketing, branding, communication and much more. She is a certified marketer whom has great zeal for helping micro and small business owners grow their business, with her wealth of knowledge and experience. Bryant-Tucker is committed to giving the best of marketing services with a focus on reasonably prices, top-quality marketing and publicity services. She is a native of Rocky Mount, North Carolina, but for the past 27 years *of her life* resided in Raleigh, North Carolina. Marilyn holds an MBA in Marketing, Executive Graduate Certificate Business Administration and has pursued Doctoral Studies in Marketing. She earned her Master's Business Administration in Marketing from Strayer University in 2011 and an Executive Graduate Certificate.

www.ingramcontent.com/pod-product-compliance
Lightning Source LLC
Chambersburg PA
CBHW070820180526
45168CB00002B/690